Activating God's Blessings Through Prophetic Declarations

26 COVENANT PROMISES FOR OPEN HEAVEN

DR. JOHN ANIEMEKE

26 COVENANT PROMISES FOR OPEN HEAVEN

Paperback ISBN: 978-1-965593-78-3

Published by Cornerstone Publishing

A Division of Cornerstone Creativity Group LLC
Info@thecornerstonepublishers.com
www.thecornerstonepublishers.com

Author's Contact

To book the author to speak at your next event or to order bulk copies of this book, please, use the information below:

janiemeke@yahoo.com

Printed in the United States of America.

This book is dedicated to the amazing **Bethel Covenant Assembly of God Global Family,** a people devoted to God and steadfast in prayer. Touching Heaven, Changing Earth.

CONTENTS

INTRODUCTION

Welcome to a life-transforming journey through God's covenant promises! This book is not just a collection of inspirational thoughts—it is a powerful declaration of what God has already promised you through His Word. Every promise in this book is backed by the unchanging nature of God, and each one is designed to position you for supernatural breakthrough.

The concept of "open heaven" is central to understanding God's covenant with you. An open heaven means unrestricted access to God's presence, provision, protection, and power. When heaven is open over your life, blessings flow freely, prayers are answered swiftly, and breakthrough manifests consistently. Jesus opened heaven for you through His death and resurrection, tearing the veil that once separated humanity from God. You are no longer waiting for heaven to open—it is already open, and these 26 covenant promises are your keys to walking in that reality.

A covenant is more than a contract or agreement. It is a sacred, unbreakable bond between God and His people. Unlike human promises that can fail, God's covenant promises are eternal, irrevocable, and guaranteed by His faithfulness. When God makes a covenant promise, He backs it with His own character. He cannot lie, He cannot fail, and He cannot change His mind. What He promises, He performs.

Throughout Scripture, God has established covenants with His people—covenants of blessing, provision, protection, multiplication, and restoration. These are not just historical events; they are living realities available to every believer today. Through Christ, you have been grafted into the family of God and have become an heir to every covenant promise. This means that what God promised Abraham, David, and the prophets is also yours by faith.

This book contains 26 covenant promises drawn directly from Scripture. Each chapter focuses on one specific covenant and its practical application to your life. You will discover promises concerning your finances, health, family, destiny, peace, joy, protection, and so much more. As you read, you will realize that God has already provided everything you need for life and godliness through these covenants.

HOW TO USE THIS BOOK

Each chapter includes a Scripture passage, a reflection on the covenant promise, and ten prophetic declarations. I encourage you to read one chapter at a time, allowing the Word of God to saturate your heart and mind. Don't rush through the chapters. Meditate on the Scriptures. Reflect on how each covenant applies to your specific situation. Then speak the prophetic declarations out loud over your life.

These declarations are not magic formulas—they are faith-filled confessions rooted in God's Word. When you declare God's promises, you are aligning your words with heaven's reality. You are speaking what God has already spoken. You are calling those things that are not as though they were, just as Abraham did. Your declarations activate your faith and position you to receive what God has already promised.

I also encourage you to revisit chapters that speak to your current season. If you're facing financial challenges, spend time in the Covenant of Supernatural Supply and the Covenant of Good Treasures and Prosperity. If you're battling fear or anxiety, meditate on the Covenant of Peace and the Covenant of Divine Protection. Let the Holy Spirit guide you to the promises you need most.

As you journey through these 26 covenant promises, expect transformation. Expect breakthrough. Expect heaven to open over your life in ways you've never experienced before. God is too faithful to fail, and His covenant promises will manifest in your life as you believe, declare, and walk in faith.

Let's begin this journey together. Your open heaven season starts now!

Dr. John C. Aniemeke

1

COVENANT OF OPEN HEAVEN BLESSINGS

"Rain down, you heavens, from above, and let the skies pour down righteousness; let the earth open, let them bring forth salvation, and let righteousness spring up together. I, the LORD, have created it."

– Isaiah 45:8 (NKJV) –

When God speaks of an open heaven, He is declaring that every barrier between you and your breakthrough has been removed. The prophet Isaiah paints a beautiful picture—the heavens dropping down blessings, the skies pouring down righteousness, and the earth opening to bring forth salvation. This is a divine orchestration of your breakthrough!

You are not waiting for heaven to open. Heaven is already open over your life because of the finished work of Jesus Christ. When Jesus died on the cross and rose again, He tore the veil that separated us from God's presence. What used to be closed is now permanently open for those who believe.

An open heaven is not just about spiritual blessings alone. Yes, God wants to pour out His Spirit upon you, but He also wants to release tangible, material blessings into your life. The text says the earth will "open and bring forth salvation." Salvation here means deliverance, provision, healing, restoration—everything you need for life and godliness.

The moment you realize you have covenant access to heaven's resources, you will stop living like a beggar and start living like a son or daughter. You have the right to expect blessings to drop down from heaven. Not because of your works, but because of your covenant relationship with God through Jesus Christ.

God is saying to you today: "I have created this open heaven blessing for you." He created it. He designed it. He ordained it before you were born. Your breakthrough is not dependent on economic conditions, political situations, or your current circumstances. It is dependent on one thing—God's covenant faithfulness.

When heaven is open over your life, things work differently. Favor will locate you in unexpected places. Opportunities will come looking for you. Resources will be released to you from sources you never imagined. People who have no reason to bless you will suddenly become instruments of your breakthrough.

The Bible says, "I the LORD have created it." When God creates something, it cannot be destroyed by the enemy. Your open heaven blessing is a divine creation that cannot be stopped by any opposition. Not by the devil. Not by negative people. Not by difficult circumstances. What God has created for you will find its way to you!

PROPHETIC DECLARATIONS

1. I declare that heaven is open over my life, and blessings are pouring down upon me from above in Jesus' name!
2. I declare that every barrier between me and my breakthrough has been permanently removed by the blood of Jesus Christ!
3. I declare that righteousness is springing up in every area of my life—my family, my finances, my health, and my destiny!
4. I declare that the earth is opening to bring forth salvation, deliverance, provision, and healing for me today!
5. I declare that I have covenant access to heaven's unlimited resources, and I receive them by faith now!

6. I declare that favor is locating me, opportunities are seeking me out, and resources are being released to me from unexpected sources!

7. I declare that what God has created for me cannot be stopped, stolen, or destroyed—my open heaven blessings are manifesting now in the mighty name of Jesus!

8. I declare that I am not a beggar but a son/daughter with full covenant access to my Father's unlimited heavenly storehouse!

9. I declare that doors are swinging open supernaturally for me, and divine opportunities are pursuing me in every direction!

10. I declare that economic conditions, political situations, and current circumstances have no power over my breakthrough—God's covenant faithfulness guarantees my success now!

In Jesus' mighty name, AMEN!

2

COVENANT OF HEAVEN ON EARTH

For the land which you go to possess is not like the land of Egypt from which you have come, where you sowed your seed and watered it by foot, as a vegetable garden; but the land which you cross over to possess is a land of hills and valleys, which drinks water from the rain of heaven, a land for which the LORD your God cares; the eyes of the LORD your God are always on it, from the beginning of the year to the very end of the year.

– Deuteronomy 11:10-12 (NKJV) –

There is a dimension in God where you don't have to struggle anymore. There is a place where heaven comes down to meet you on earth. This is what Moses was revealing to the children of Israel as they prepared to enter the Promised Land. He said, "Where you're going is not like where you've been."

In Egypt, they had to water their crops "with their foot"—meaning they had to work hard, labor intensely, and use human effort to make things happen. But in the land God was taking them to, heaven itself would water their land. They would drink water from the rain of heaven. Can you see the difference? One requires human struggle; the other requires divine partnership.

Many believers today are still living in "Egypt mode." They are watering their dreams, their businesses, their families, and their ministries with their own foot—with human effort alone. They are exhausted, burned out, and frustrated because nothing seems to be working despite all their hard work. But God is calling you out of Egypt and into a land where heaven comes down to bless your efforts!

The text says something powerful: "The eyes of the LORD your God are always on it, from the beginning of the year to the very end of the year." Did you catch that? God's eyes are always upon your Promised Land. From the beginning of the year to the end of the year, God is watching over your inheritance. He is monitoring your progress. He is orchestrating your breakthrough. You are never out of His sight!

When heaven comes down to earth, the impossible becomes possible. The difficult becomes easy. The closed becomes open. Things that should take years to accomplish happen in months or even days. Why? Because heaven is backing you up!

God wants you to stop struggling and start receiving. He wants you to stop watering your life with your foot and start positioning yourself to receive rain from heaven. How do you do this? By faith. By believing that God cares for your land. By trusting that His eyes are upon your situation. By expecting heaven to invade your circumstances.

Today, heaven is coming down to meet you where you are. The rain of blessing is about to fall on your life. What you have labored for with little results is about to produce a supernatural harvest. God's eyes are upon you, and He is about to show you that He cares deeply for everything that concerns you!

PROPHETIC DECLARATIONS

1. I declare that I am leaving "Egypt mode" behind and stepping into the land where heaven waters my efforts with supernatural blessings!

2. I declare that I am done struggling with my own strength—heaven is partnering with me to produce abundant fruit in every area of my life!

3. I declare that the LORD cares for my land, and His eyes are always upon my life, my family, my work, and my destiny!

4. I declare that heaven is raining blessings upon everything I put my hands to, and I am experiencing supernatural increase!

5. I declare that what should take years to accomplish is happening in months and days because heaven is backing me up!

6. I declare that the impossible is becoming possible, the difficult is becoming easy, and closed doors are swinging open before me!

7. I declare that I am receiving rain from heaven—divine provision, divine connections, divine opportunities, and divine favor—now in Jesus' name!

8. I declare that supernatural harvests are manifesting in areas where I have labored with little results—my season of abundance has come!

9. I declare that I am positioning myself to receive, not struggle, and heaven is invading my circumstances with miracles right now!

10. I declare that from the beginning of this year to the end of this year, God's eyes are continuously upon me, orchestrating my breakthrough and watching over my destiny!

In Jesus' mighty name, AMEN!

3

COVENANT OF PEACE

Moreover I will make a covenant of peace with them, and it shall be an everlasting covenant with them; I will establish them and multiply them, and I will set My sanctuary in their midst forevermore.

– Ezekiel 37:26 (NKJV) –

Peace is not just the absence of trouble; peace is the presence of God's perfect order in your life. When God speaks of making a covenant of peace with you, He is declaring that no matter what storm is raging around you, you will experience His supernatural calm and divine order within you.

The Hebrew word for peace is "shalom," and it means so much more than we often understand. Shalom means completeness, wholeness, safety, prosperity, rest, and harmony. It means nothing is missing and nothing is broken in your life. This is the kind of peace God has covenanted with you—a peace that makes you whole in every area.

Notice something critical in this passage: God says, "I will make a covenant of peace with them." God initiates this covenant. You don't have to beg for it, earn it, or qualify for it. God has already decided to establish peace in your life. Your part is simply to receive it by faith and walk in it daily.

The Bible says in Philippians 4:7, "And the peace of God, which surpasses all understanding, will guard your hearts and minds through Christ Jesus" (NKJV). This peace guards you. It protects you. It keeps you stable when everything around you is unstable. This is covenant peace!

God says this covenant of peace is "everlasting." It is not temporary. It is not conditional on your circumstances. It is permanent because it is rooted in God's unchanging nature. When your job is unstable, your peace remains. When your health is threatened, your peace remains. When relationships are difficult, your peace remains. Why? Because your peace is not based on what's happening around you but on who lives inside you!

God also promises, "I will set My sanctuary in their midst forevermore." A sanctuary is a holy place where God dwells. God is saying that He will make His home in the middle of your life. When God's presence is in the center of your life, peace is automatic. His presence drives out fear, anxiety, depression, and confusion.

The devil's greatest weapon against believers is not poverty or sickness—it is the loss of peace. When the enemy can steal your peace, he can control your decisions, paralyze your faith, and limit your effectiveness. But when you guard your covenant of peace, you remain in a position of power and authority.

Today, take inventory of your life. Where have you allowed the enemy to steal your peace? What situation is robbing you of your rest? It's time to reclaim your covenant right! God has already made peace with you. You don't need to create peace—you need to receive the peace that already belongs to you. Let the peace of God flood your heart and silence every fear!

PROPHETIC DECLARATIONS

1. I declare that the Covenant of Peace is established in my life, and nothing is missing and nothing is broken in me!
2. I declare that supernatural peace floods my heart and mind, and I am walking in divine order in every area of my life!

3. I declare that God's presence is the sanctuary in the midst of my life, and His peace guards me against every attack of the enemy!

4. I declare that my peace is not temporary or conditional—it is everlasting and rooted in God's unchanging nature!

5. I declare that I refuse to allow fear, anxiety, or worry to steal my covenant right of peace in Jesus' name!

6. I declare that shalom—completeness, wholeness, safety, prosperity, and rest—is manifesting in my family, my health, my finances, and my destiny!

7. I declare that I am walking in the peace that passes all understanding, and every storm around me must bow to the calm within me now!

8. I declare that I am reclaiming my covenant right of peace from every situation, worry, and circumstance that has tried to steal it!

9. I declare that the devil's weapon of fear, anxiety, and worry is powerless against me—I guard my peace and remain in a position of power and authority!

10. I declare that God's sanctuary is established in the midst of my life, and His presence is driving out every form of fear, confusion, and torment in Jesus' mighty name!

In Jesus' mighty name, AMEN!

4

COVENANT OF SUPERNATURAL SUPPLY

But seek first the kingdom of God and His righteousness, and all these things shall be added to you.

– Matthew 6:33 (NKJV) –

God's provision for your life is not based on the economy, your job security, or your bank account. It is based on a covenant promise that when you prioritize His kingdom, He will supernaturally supply all your needs. This is the divine exchange—you give God first place, and He takes responsibility for everything else in your life.

Jesus spoke these words to people who were worried about food, clothing, and basic necessities. He didn't dismiss their concerns as unimportant. Instead, He revealed a kingdom principle: seek first the kingdom of God, and watch everything you need pursue you. Notice the word "added"—it means things will be given to you without you chasing after them.

Many believers struggle financially because they have reversed God's order. They seek provision first and give God whatever is left over. But God says, "Put Me first, and I will ensure that provision finds you." This is not about neglecting your responsibilities; it's about trusting that when you honor God with your priorities, He will honor you with His provision.

The phrase "all these things" is comprehensive. It includes your daily needs, your unexpected expenses, your future requirements, and even your desires. God is not a minimalist who only provides bare necessities. He is a generous Father who delights in blessing His children abundantly.

When you operate under the Covenant of Supernatural Supply, you will experience provision that defies natural explanation. Money will come from unexpected sources. Opportunities will open up suddenly. Debts will be canceled. Needs will be met before you even ask. This is how God operates when His kingdom takes first place in your life.

The key is consistency. Seeking God's kingdom first is not a one-time decision; it's a daily lifestyle. It means making choices that honor God even when they don't make financial sense. It means tithing and giving even when your account is low. It means trusting God's timing even when bills are due. When you live this way, you activate the Covenant of Supernatural Supply, and God becomes responsible for your provision.

PROPHETIC DECLARATIONS

1. I declare that I am seeking first the kingdom of God and His righteousness, and all things I need are being added to me now!
2. I declare that God's supernatural supply is activated in my life, and provision is pursuing me from every direction!
3. I declare that my financial breakthrough is not dependent on the economy, my job, or my circumstances—it is dependent on God's covenant faithfulness!
4. I declare that money is coming to me from unexpected sources, and opportunities are opening up suddenly for my benefit!
5. I declare that debts are being canceled, needs are being met before I ask, and abundance is replacing lack in my life!
6. I declare that I am not chasing after provision—provision is chasing after me because I have made God's kingdom my priority!

7. I declare that God takes full responsibility for my provision when I put Him first, and He is supplying all my needs according to His riches in glory!

8. I declare that I am breaking free from the spirit of lack and entering into the realm of supernatural supply and abundance!

9. I declare that my obedience in tithing, giving, and honoring God is opening the windows of heaven over my finances!

10. I declare that I am walking in the Covenant of Supernatural Supply, and everything I need for life and godliness is being added to me now in Jesus' name!

In Jesus' mighty name, AMEN!

5

COVENANT OF DEFENSE AND DELIVERANCE

"For I," says the LORD, "will be a wall of fire all around her, and I will be the glory in her midst."

– Zechariah 2:5 (NKJV) –

God is not only your provider; He is also your protector. The Covenant of Defense and Deliverance guarantees that you are surrounded by divine protection every moment of every day. God Himself becomes a wall of fire around you—an impenetrable barrier that no enemy can cross.

Fire is both protective and destructive. As a wall of fire around you, God's presence shields you from harm while simultaneously consuming every attack launched against you. This means that every weapon formed against you will not prosper, and every tongue that rises against you in judgment will be condemned. You are not fighting alone; God is fighting for you.

Notice that God says He will be "the glory in her midst." This means that while God protects you from external attacks, He also fills you with His presence from within. You are not just defended; you are indwelt. The same God who surrounds you also sustains you. This is complete protection—external defense and internal strength.

Many believers live in constant fear of what the enemy might do. They worry about spiritual attacks, physical harm, financial loss, and relational betrayal. But when you understand the Covenant of Defense and Deliverance, fear has no place in your life. You are not vulnerable. You are not exposed. You are surrounded by the Almighty God who never sleeps, never fails, and never loses a battle.

This covenant also includes deliverance. God doesn't just protect you from future attacks; He delivers you from present bondages. Whatever has held you captive—addiction, depression, fear, poverty, sickness—God is breaking those chains right now. The same fire that defends you also sets you free.

Walking in this covenant requires faith and boldness. You must refuse to live in fear and instead stand on God's promises. When threats come, declare God's protection. When attacks arise, trust God's defense. When bondage tries to return, claim your deliverance. You are not a victim; you are victorious through Christ who strengthens you!

PROPHETIC DECLARATIONS

1. I declare that God is a wall of fire around me, and no weapon formed against me shall prosper!
2. I declare that every attack launched against my life, family, health, and finances is consumed by the fire of God's presence!
3. I declare that I am not vulnerable or exposed—I am surrounded by the Almighty God who fights for me!
4. I declare that God is the glory in my midst, filling me with His strength, courage, and peace from within!
5. I declare that every tongue that rises against me in judgment is condemned, and I am vindicated by the Lord!
6. I declare that fear has no place in my life because I walk under the Covenant of Defense and Deliverance!
7. I declare that I am delivered from every bondage—addiction, depression, fear, poverty, and sickness—by the power of God!
8. I declare that the same fire that defends me also sets me free, and I am walking in complete victory today!

9. I declare that I refuse to live as a victim—I am victorious through Christ who strengthens me and fights my battles!

10. I declare that God never sleeps, never fails, and never loses a battle, and His protection is upon me 24 hours a day, 7 days a week, in Jesus' name!

In Jesus' mighty name, AMEN!

6

COVENANT OF DIVINE PROTECTION

As the mountains surround Jerusalem, so the LORD surrounds His people from this time forth and forever.

– Psalm 125:2 (NKJV) –

The imagery in this verse is powerful and permanent. Just as mountains surround Jerusalem providing natural protection, God surrounds His people with divine protection that cannot be moved, shaken, or penetrated. This is not temporary security; this is eternal protection—from this time forth and forever.

Mountains are immovable, unshakeable, and unchanging. They don't shift with the seasons or crumble with the storms. They stand firm year after year, generation after generation. This is how God's protection works in your life. It doesn't fluctuate based on your circumstances.

It doesn't weaken when you're going through trials. It remains constant because it is rooted in God's unchanging nature.

What makes this covenant even more remarkable is that God doesn't send protection—He becomes your protection. The verse says "the LORD surrounds His people." Not angels, not circumstances, not human effort—the LORD Himself. When you have God surrounding you, you have the most secure protection available in the universe.

This divine protection covers every area of your life. Your mind is protected from confusion and deception. Your heart is protected from bitterness and offense. Your body is protected from sickness and harm. Your family is protected from division and destruction. Your finances are protected from loss and poverty. Your destiny is protected from delay and derailment. Nothing in your life is left unguarded.

Some people believe that walking with God means you'll never face challenges. That's not true. The mountains around Jerusalem didn't prevent attacks; they made the city difficult to conquer. Similarly, God's protection doesn't mean you won't face battles, but it does mean you won't be defeated. Every challenge you face will ultimately work for your good because you are surrounded by divine protection.

Today, take comfort in knowing that you are not navigating life alone. You are surrounded—front, back, left, right, above, and below—by the presence of Almighty God. No attack can reach you without going through Him first, and nothing gets through God!

PROPHETIC DECLARATIONS

1. I declare that the LORD surrounds me like mountains surround Jerusalem, and I am protected from this time forth and forever!
2. I declare that God's protection over my life is immovable, unshakeable, and unchanging—it remains constant regardless of my circumstances!
3. I declare that God Himself is my protection, and when I have Him surrounding me, I have the most secure protection in the universe!
4. I declare that my mind is protected from confusion, my heart is protected from bitterness, and my body is protected from sickness and harm!
5. I declare that my family is protected from division, my finances are protected from loss, and my destiny is protected from delay!
6. I declare that no area of my life is left unguarded—everything I am and everything I have is covered by divine protection!

7. I declare that every battle I face will ultimately work for my good because I am surrounded by God's presence!

8. I declare that no attack can reach me without going through God first, and nothing gets through Him!

9. I declare that I am not navigating life alone—God is surrounding me front, back, left, right, above, and below with His mighty hand!

10. I declare that I walk in complete security and confidence because the Covenant of Divine Protection is activated over my life right now in Jesus' name!

In Jesus' mighty name, AMEN!

7

COVENANT OF LONG LIFE AND BEST OF DAYS

"He shall call upon Me, and I will answer him; I will be with him in trouble; I will deliver him and honor him. With long life I will satisfy him, and show him My salvation."

– Psalm 91:15-16 (NKJV) –

God's plan for your life includes longevity and quality. The Covenant of Long Life and Best of Days is not just about the number of years you live, but about the satisfaction and fulfillment you experience in those years. God wants you to live long and live well.

Notice the progression in these verses: God answers when you call, He stays with you in trouble, He delivers you from danger, He honors you publicly, He satisfies you with long life, and He shows you His salvation. This is a comprehensive covenant that covers every aspect of your existence from beginning to end.

The promise of long life is conditional on one thing—calling upon God. When you maintain a relationship with Him, when you pray, when you seek His face, when you trust His Word, you activate this covenant. Long life is not automatic for everyone, but it is guaranteed for those who walk closely with God.

But this covenant goes beyond just living many years. The word "satisfy" is key. God will satisfy you with long life, meaning your days will be full, meaningful, and purposeful. You won't just exist; you'll thrive. You won't just survive; you'll flourish. Your latter days will be greater than your former days.

Many people live long but are not satisfied. They have years but no joy. They have age but no fulfillment. But God's covenant includes both longevity and satisfaction. He gives you the years and fills those years with His goodness, His blessings, His presence, and His purpose.

The phrase "and show him My salvation" means that you will see God's deliverance, healing, and breakthrough throughout your life. You won't die prematurely. You won't be cut off in your prime. You will live to see your children's children, accomplish your purpose, and finish your assignment on earth with joy and satisfaction.

Today, declare that premature death has no claim on you. Sickness cannot shorten your days. Accidents cannot derail your destiny. You are covered by the Covenant of Long Life and Best of Days, and you will live to fulfill everything God has called you to do!

PROPHETIC DECLARATIONS

1. I declare that I am walking in the Covenant of Long Life and Best of Days, and I will live long and live well!
2. I declare that God answers when I call, stays with me in trouble, delivers me from danger, and honors me publicly!
3. I declare that my life is not just about the number of years I live but about the satisfaction and fulfillment I experience in those years!
4. I declare that I am calling upon God daily, and I am activating the covenant of long life over my destiny!
5. I declare that God is satisfying me with long life—my days are full, meaningful, and purposeful in Him!
6. I declare that I will not just exist—I will thrive! I will not just survive—I will flourish! My latter days will be greater than my former days!

7. I declare that premature death has no claim on me, and I am breaking every curse of early death off my bloodline!

8. I declare that sickness cannot shorten my days, accidents cannot derail my destiny, and I will live to fulfill my purpose on earth!

9. I declare that I will see my children's children, accomplish every assignment God has given me, and finish my race with joy!

10. I declare that I will live to see God's salvation, deliverance, healing, and breakthrough throughout my life in Jesus' mighty name!

In Jesus' mighty name, AMEN!

8

COVENANT OF GRACE

And of His fullness we have all received, and grace for grace.

– John 1:16 (NKJV) –

Grace is not just unmerited favor; it is God's divine enablement to do what you cannot do in your own strength. The Covenant of Grace guarantees that you have unlimited access to God's ability, power, and resources to accomplish everything He has called you to do.

John reveals something profound here: "Of His fullness we have all received." This means that Christ's fullness has been made available to you. Everything Jesus has—His wisdom, His authority, His power, His anointing, His righteousness—has been transferred to you through grace. You are not lacking anything!

The phrase "grace for grace" literally means "grace upon grace" or "one grace after another." It's like waves of the ocean—just when one wave of grace finishes its work in your life, another wave is already on its way. God's grace never runs out. It keeps coming, wave after wave, empowering you for every challenge, every opportunity, and every season.

Many believers struggle unnecessarily because they try to accomplish God's purposes in their own strength. They work hard, strive endlessly, and still fall short. But grace changes everything. When you operate in grace, difficult things become easy. Impossible tasks become possible. Heavy burdens become light. Why? Because it's not you doing it—it's God's grace working through you.

This covenant applies to every area of your life. You need grace for your marriage, grace for your children, grace for your business, grace for your ministry, grace for your health, and grace for your finances. The good news is that all these graces are available to you right now through Christ.

The key to walking in grace is acknowledging your dependence on God. Grace flows to the humble, those who recognize they cannot succeed without God's help. When you stop striving and start receiving, when you stop struggling and start trusting, when you stop working in the flesh and start walking in the Spirit—grace floods your life like a river.

Today, receive fresh grace for whatever you're facing. Whether you're dealing with relationships, finances, health, or ministry, declare that God's grace is sufficient for you. His strength is made perfect in your weakness, and His grace is more than enough to carry you through!

PROPHETIC DECLARATIONS

1. I declare that I have received of Christ's fullness, and I lack nothing that I need for life and godliness!
2. I declare that grace upon grace is flowing into my life like waves of the ocean—one grace after another, continuously empowering me!
3. I declare that everything Jesus has—His wisdom, authority, power, anointing, and righteousness—has been transferred to me through grace!
4. I declare that I am not struggling in my own strength—God's grace is working through me, making the difficult easy and the impossible possible!
5. I declare that I have grace for my marriage, grace for my children, grace for my business, grace for my health, and grace for my finances!
6. I declare that heavy burdens are becoming light, overwhelming tasks are becoming manageable, and God's grace is sufficient for me!

7. I declare that I am stopping the striving and receiving God's grace, trusting His strength instead of relying on my own!

8. I declare that God's strength is made perfect in my weakness, and His grace is more than enough to carry me through every challenge!

9. I declare that grace flows to the humble, and I acknowledge my complete dependence on God for everything in my life!

10. I declare that I am walking in the Covenant of Grace, and fresh grace is flooding my life right now for everything I'm facing in Jesus' name!

In Jesus' mighty name, AMEN!

9

COVENANT OF GLORY

"The glory of this latter temple shall be greater than the former," says the LORD of hosts. "And in this place I will give peace," says the LORD of hosts.

– Haggai 2:9 (NKJV) –

God specializes in making your latter greater than your former. The Covenant of Glory guarantees that no matter what you've lost, no matter what season you've been through, your future will surpass your past. Your best days are not behind you—they are ahead of you!

The prophet Haggai spoke these words to a discouraged people who were rebuilding the temple. The older generation remembered the glory of Solomon's temple and wept because the new temple seemed inferior. But God declared that the glory of the latter temple would exceed the former. What seemed like a downgrade was actually an upgrade in God's plan.

Many believers are discouraged because their present situation doesn't match their past experiences. They remember better days—more money, better health, stronger relationships, greater influence—and they wonder if they'll ever experience glory again. But God is saying, "Your latter glory will be greater than your former glory!"

This covenant means that setbacks are setups for comebacks. Losses are setups for greater gains. Delays are setups for divine acceleration. Failures are setups for future success. What the enemy meant for evil, God will turn around for your good, and you will emerge with more glory than you had before.

The promise includes peace: "And in this place I will give peace." Not only will your glory increase, but you will also have peace in the process. You won't be anxious about your future because you know God is orchestrating your comeback. You won't be bitter about your past because you understand that everything you went through was preparing you for greater glory.

This is not just about material blessings, though those are included. This is about the manifestation of God's presence, power, and purpose in your life at a greater level than ever before. Your latter glory includes deeper intimacy with God, greater influence, increased anointing, expanded territory, and supernatural favor.

Today, lift up your head! Your mourning is turning into dancing. Your ashes are becoming beauty. Your losses are becoming testimonies. The Covenant of Glory is activated over your life, and your best is yet to come!

PROPHETIC DECLARATIONS

1. I declare that the glory of my latter days will be greater than the glory of my former days—my best is yet to come!
2. I declare that what seems like a downgrade in my life right now is actually an upgrade in God's plan for me!
3. I declare that every setback I've experienced is a setup for a supernatural comeback greater than anything I've seen before!
4. I declare that my losses are being turned into greater gains, my delays into divine acceleration, and my failures into future success!
5. I declare that what the enemy meant for evil, God is turning around for my good, and I will emerge with more glory than before!
6. I declare that I am not anxious about my future because God is orchestrating my comeback with greater glory!

7. I declare that I refuse to be bitter about my past—everything I went through was preparing me for this season of greater glory!

8. I declare that my latter glory includes deeper intimacy with God, greater influence, increased anointing, and supernatural favor!

9. I declare that my mourning is turning into dancing, my ashes are becoming beauty, and my losses are becoming powerful testimonies!

10. I declare that the Covenant of Glory is activated over my life right now, and I am stepping into the greatest season I've ever experienced in Jesus' mighty name!

In Jesus' mighty name, AMEN!

10

COVENANT OF MERCY

But Zion said, "The LORD has forsaken me, and my Lord has forgotten me." "Can a woman forget her nursing child, and not have compassion on the son of her womb? Surely they may forget, yet I will not forget you."

– Isaiah 49:13-15 (NKJV) –

God's mercy toward you is deeper than any human love and more enduring than any earthly relationship. The Covenant of Mercy assures you that God has not forgotten you, He has not forsaken you, and He will never abandon you—no matter what you're going through.

The people of Israel felt abandoned by God. They believed He had forgotten their suffering and forsaken their cause. But God's response is powerful: He compares His love to a mother's love for her nursing child. A mother cannot forget her baby who depends on her for nourishment and care. Even if she could forget—which is nearly impossible—God says, "I will not forget you."

This covenant is for those moments when you feel invisible, overlooked, and abandoned. When your prayers seem unanswered, when your situation seems hopeless, when everyone else has moved on, God is still there. He sees you. He knows you. He remembers you. His mercy is pursuing you even when you can't sense it.

Mercy means God gives you what you don't deserve and withholds what you do deserve. You deserve judgment, but He gives you grace. You deserve condemnation, but He gives you forgiveness. You deserve rejection, but He gives you acceptance. This is the nature of God's mercy—it's unmerited, unconditional, and unending.

The Covenant of Mercy also means that God's compassion toward you is renewed every morning. Yesterday's failures don't define today's opportunities. Last year's mistakes don't limit this year's miracles. God's mercies are new every morning, and His faithfulness is great toward you.

When you walk in this covenant, you experience divine compassion in your darkest moments. You receive second chances when you've failed. You find hope when everything seems hopeless. You encounter God's kindness when you least expect it. This is mercy—God meeting you in your mess and lifting you into His purpose.

Today, receive fresh mercy for your situation. Whatever you're facing—past mistakes, present struggles, or future fears—God's mercy is greater. He has not forgotten you. He has not forsaken you. He is with you, and His mercy will carry you through!

PROPHETIC DECLARATIONS

1. I declare that God has not forgotten me, He has not forsaken me, and He will never abandon me no matter what I'm facing!
2. I declare that God's mercy toward me is deeper than any human love and more enduring than any earthly relationship!
3. I declare that even when I feel invisible and overlooked, God sees me, knows me, remembers me, and His mercy is pursuing me!
4. I declare that God is giving me what I don't deserve—grace instead of judgment, forgiveness instead of condemnation, and acceptance instead of rejection!
5. I declare that yesterday's failures don't define today's opportunities, and last year's mistakes don't limit this year's miracles!
6. I declare that God's mercies are new every morning, and His faithfulness is great toward me in every season of my life!

7. I declare that I am receiving second chances when I've failed and finding hope when everything seems hopeless!

8. I declare that God is meeting me in my mess and lifting me into His purpose through His abundant mercy!

9. I declare that God's mercy is greater than my past mistakes, present struggles, and future fears—nothing is beyond His compassion!

10. I declare that the Covenant of Mercy is covering me right now, and fresh mercy is flowing into my situation, bringing breakthrough and restoration in Jesus' name!

In Jesus' mighty name, AMEN!

11

COVENANT OF GOOD TREASURES AND PROSPERITY

The LORD will open to you His good treasure, the heavens, to give the rain to your land in its season, and to bless all the work of your hand. You shall lend to many nations, but you shall not borrow.

– Deuteronomy 28:12 (NKJV) –

God has a storehouse of blessings with your name on it. The Covenant of Good Treasures and Prosperity declares that heaven's resources are available to you, and God Himself will open His treasure to meet your needs and fulfill your destiny.

Notice that God doesn't give you a little from His treasure—He opens the treasure to you. This means unlimited access to divine resources. You're not limited by what you can see in the natural; you're connected to what's available in the heavenly realm. When God opens His treasure, lack becomes abundance, poverty becomes prosperity, and insufficiency becomes overflow.

The text mentions two specific blessings: rain in its season and blessing on the work of your hands. Rain represents provision that comes at the right time, in the right amount, for the right purpose. God's timing is perfect, and His provision is precise. You won't get too much too soon or too little too late—you'll get exactly what you need when you need it.

The blessing on the work of your hands means that whatever you do will prosper. Your business will succeed. Your career will advance. Your investments will multiply. Your efforts will produce results. This is not about working harder; it's about working smarter under God's blessing. When God blesses the work of your hands, a little becomes much, and ordinary efforts produce extraordinary results.

The covenant also includes financial freedom: "You shall lend to many nations, but you shall not borrow." This means you will move from being in debt to being a lender, from needing help to providing help, from lack to abundance. You will have more than enough to meet your needs and enough left over to bless others.

Walking in this covenant requires obedience and stewardship. When you honor God with your finances through tithing and giving, you position yourself to receive from His treasure. When you are faithful with little, God entrusts you with much. When you use your resources to bless others, God releases His resources to bless you.

Today, declare that you are moving from borrowing to lending, from lack to abundance, from barely enough to more than enough. God's good treasure is opened over your life, and prosperity is your portion!

PROPHETIC DECLARATIONS

1. I declare that God is opening His good treasure over my life, and I have unlimited access to divine resources!
2. I declare that heaven's storehouse is available to me, and lack is becoming abundance, poverty is becoming prosperity, and insufficiency is becoming overflow!
3. I declare that rain is falling in my season—God's provision is coming at the right time, in the right amount, for the right purpose!
4. I declare that God is blessing the work of my hands, and whatever I do is prospering supernaturally!
5. I declare that my business is succeeding, my career is advancing, my investments are multiplying, and my efforts are producing extraordinary results!

6. I declare that I am moving from borrowing to lending, from needing help to providing help, from lack to abundance!

7. I declare that I have more than enough to meet my needs and enough left over to be a blessing to others!

8. I declare that as I honor God with my finances through tithing and giving, His treasure is being released into my life!

9. I declare that I am faithful with little, and God is entrusting me with much—financial increase is mine in Jesus' name!

10. I declare that the Covenant of Good Treasures and Prosperity is activated over my life, and I am walking in divine abundance right now!

In Jesus' mighty name, AMEN!

12

COVENANT OF HEALTH AND SOUND MIND

Beloved, I pray that you may prosper in all things and be in health, just as your soul prospers.

– 3 John 1:2 (NKJV) –

God's will for you is not just spiritual prosperity but total prosperity—spirit, soul, and body. The Covenant of Health and Sound Mind guarantees that God desires you to be healthy physically, stable emotionally, and sound mentally. You were not created to be sick, broken, or tormented.

This verse reveals a powerful principle: your physical health is connected to the prosperity of your soul. When your soul prospers—when your mind is renewed, your emotions are healed, and your will is aligned with God's—your body follows. Health is not just about treating symptoms; it's about addressing the root issues in your soul.

Many believers struggle with sickness and mental instability because they have not dealt with unforgiveness, bitterness, fear, anxiety, and past traumas. These soul issues manifest as physical and mental problems. But when you allow God to heal your soul through His Word, forgiveness, and the Holy Spirit's power, your body receives healing and your mind experiences peace.

The Covenant of Health and Sound Mind includes divine healing for every sickness and disease. By the stripes of Jesus, you were healed—past tense. Healing is not something you're trying to get; it's something you already have. Your responsibility is to receive it by faith and walk in it daily.

This covenant also includes mental and emotional stability. You don't have to live with depression, anxiety, fear, or confusion. God has not given you a spirit of fear but of power, love, and a sound mind. Your mind can be clear, focused, peaceful, and filled with the knowledge of God's will.

Walking in this covenant requires intentionality. You must feed your soul with God's Word, protect your mind from negative influences, guard your heart from toxic relationships, and take care of your body as the temple of the Holy Spirit. When you honor God with your body and soul, He honors you with health and wholeness.

Today, declare that sickness has no dominion over you. Mental instability has no claim on you. Emotional turmoil has no place in you. You are healed, whole, and sound in Jesus' name!

PROPHETIC DECLARATIONS

1. I declare that God's will for me is total prosperity—spirit, soul, and body—and I am walking in complete health and wholeness!
2. I declare that as my soul prospers through God's Word, my physical body is receiving healing and strength!
3. I declare that I am addressing every soul issue—unforgiveness, bitterness, fear, and past trauma—and my body and mind are being healed!
4. I declare that by the stripes of Jesus, I was healed, and I am receiving divine healing for every sickness and disease in my body!
5. I declare that I don't have to live with depression, anxiety, fear, or confusion—God has given me power, love, and a sound mind!
6. I declare that my mind is clear, focused, peaceful, and filled with the knowledge of God's will for my life!

7. I declare that I am feeding my soul with God's Word, protecting my mind from negativity, and guarding my heart from toxicity!

8. I declare that my body is the temple of the Holy Spirit, and I honor God with how I treat it physically, emotionally, and mentally!

9. I declare that sickness has no dominion over me, mental instability has no claim on me, and emotional turmoil has no place in me!

10. I declare that I am healed, whole, and sound in spirit, soul, and body—the Covenant of Health and Sound Mind is mine in Jesus' name!

In Jesus' mighty name, AMEN!

13

COVENANT OF FLOURISHING

The righteous shall flourish like a palm tree, he shall grow like a cedar in Lebanon. Those who are planted in the house of the LORD shall flourish in the courts of our God. They shall still bear fruit in old age; they shall be fresh and flourishing.

– Psalm 92:12-15 (NKJV) –

God's plan for you is not just survival—it's flourishing. The Covenant of Flourishing guarantees that you will thrive in every season of your life, producing fruit consistently from your youth to your old age.

The psalmist uses two powerful images: the palm tree and the cedar of Lebanon. The palm tree is known for its ability to thrive in harsh conditions. It bends in storms but doesn't break. It grows deep roots that tap into hidden water sources, so it stays green even in drought. The cedar of Lebanon is known for its strength, durability, and fragrance. It grows tall and majestic, providing shade and shelter.

This is how you will flourish—like a palm tree that withstands every storm and like a cedar that grows strong and majestic. You are not at the mercy of your circumstances. You are planted in the house of the Lord, and that positioning guarantees your flourishing.

The key phrase is "planted in the house of the LORD." Flourishing is not automatic for everyone; it's guaranteed for those who are planted—rooted, committed, and connected—in God's house. When you are planted in a local church, submitted to spiritual leadership, engaged in corporate worship, and serving faithfully, you position yourself for supernatural flourishing.

Notice that flourishing is not limited by age. The text says, "They shall still bear fruit in old age; they shall be fresh and flourishing." Many people decline as they age, but God's covenant declares that you will remain productive, vibrant, and fruitful throughout your life. Your latter years will not be marked by decline but by increase.

Flourishing includes every area of your life—spiritual growth, financial increase, relational health, physical vitality, and ministry fruitfulness. You will not plateau or stagnate. You will continue to grow, expand, increase, and produce fruit that remains.

Today, declare that you are not just surviving—you are flourishing! You are not withering—you are thriving! You are not declining—you are increasing! The Covenant of Flourishing is activated over your life, and you will bear fruit in every season!

PROPHETIC DECLARATIONS

1. I declare that I am not just surviving—I am flourishing in every season of my life!
2. I declare that I am like a palm tree that bends in storms but doesn't break and like a cedar that grows strong and majestic!
3. I declare that I am not at the mercy of my circumstances—I am planted in the house of the LORD, and my flourishing is guaranteed!
4. I declare that I am rooted, committed, and connected in God's house, and I am positioned for supernatural flourishing!
5. I declare that my flourishing is not limited by age—I will remain productive, vibrant, and fruitful throughout my entire life!

6. I declare that my latter years will not be marked by decline but by increase—I will bear fruit in old age!

7. I declare that I am flourishing spiritually, financially, relationally, physically, and in ministry—every area of my life is thriving!

8. I declare that I am not plateauing or stagnating—I am continuing to grow, expand, increase, and produce fruit that remains!

9. I declare that like a palm tree, I have deep roots that tap into God's hidden resources, so I stay fresh even in drought!

10. I declare that the Covenant of Flourishing is activated over my life right now, and I am bearing fruit in every season in Jesus' mighty name!

In Jesus' mighty name, AMEN!

14

COVENANT OF MIGHT

So David inquired of the LORD, saying, "Shall I pursue this troop? Shall I overtake them?" And He answered him, "Pursue, for you shall surely overtake them and without fail recover all."

– 1 Samuel 30:8 (NKJV) –

The Covenant of Might is God's promise that you have divine strength to pursue, overtake, and recover everything the enemy has stolen from you. You are not powerless against the attacks of darkness. You are empowered by the Almighty to fight back and win!

David was in a desperate situation. His city had been burned, his families had been kidnapped, and his men wanted to stone him. But instead of giving up, David inquired of the Lord and received a powerful promise: "Pursue, for you shall surely overtake them and without fail recover all." This is the same promise God is giving you today.

The phrase "without fail recover all" is comprehensive. Not some things. Not most things. ALL things. Everything the enemy has stolen—your peace, your joy, your health, your finances, your relationships, your destiny—can be recovered. Nothing is lost forever when you walk in the Covenant of Might.

But notice that recovery requires action. God told David to "pursue." You cannot sit passively and expect your breakthrough to fall into your lap. You must rise up in faith, take authority over the enemy, and pursue what belongs to you. This is not about physical fighting; it's about spiritual warfare through prayer, declaration, and faith-filled action.

The Covenant of Might gives you supernatural strength to fight battles you couldn't win in your own power. When you are weak, He makes you strong. When you are tired, He renews your strength. When you are overwhelmed, He becomes your fortress. His might is made available to you through His Spirit living in you.

This covenant also includes divine strategy. Just as God gave David specific instructions on when and how to pursue, He will give you wisdom for your battles. You don't have to figure everything out on your own. God will show you the right time to advance, the right path to take, and the right weapons to use.

Today, stop mourning over what you've lost and start pursuing what God has promised to restore. Rise up in the Covenant of Might, take authority over the enemy, and declare that you will overtake and recover all in Jesus' name!

PROPHETIC DECLARATIONS

1. I declare that I have divine strength to pursue, overtake, and recover everything the enemy has stolen from me!
2. I declare that I am not powerless against the attacks of darkness—I am empowered by the Almighty to fight back and win!
3. I declare that I will without fail recover all—my peace, my joy, my health, my finances, my relationships, and my destiny!
4. I declare that nothing is lost forever when I walk in the Covenant of Might—everything stolen is being restored right now!
5. I declare that I am rising up in faith, taking authority over the enemy, and pursuing everything that belongs to me!
6. I declare that when I am weak, God makes me strong; when I am tired, He renews my strength; when I am overwhelmed, He becomes my fortress!

7. I declare that God is giving me divine strategy for my battles—He is showing me when to advance, which path to take, and which weapons to use!

8. I declare that I am not mourning over what I've lost—I am pursuing what God has promised to restore!

9. I declare that supernatural strength is flowing into me right now, and I am fighting battles I couldn't win in my own power!

10. I declare that I am walking in the Covenant of Might, taking authority over every attack, and recovering all in Jesus' mighty name!

In Jesus' mighty name, AMEN!

15

COVENANT OF PRAISE AND THANKSGIVING

Enter into His gates with thanksgiving, and into His courts with praise. Be thankful to Him, and bless His name.

– Psalm 100:4 (NKJV) –

Praise and thanksgiving are not just religious activities—they are covenant keys that unlock God's presence, power, and provision in your life. The Covenant of Praise and Thanksgiving guarantees that when you worship God with a grateful heart, you gain access to His courts where miracles happen.

Notice the progression: you enter His gates with thanksgiving and move into His courts with praise. Thanksgiving is the entry point, and praise takes you deeper into God's presence. When you begin to thank God for what He has already done, your heart opens to praise Him for who He is. This combination of thanksgiving and praise positions you for breakthrough.

Many believers struggle with worry, fear, and anxiety because they focus on their problems instead of God's faithfulness. But when you shift your focus from your circumstances to God's goodness through thanksgiving, everything changes. Thanksgiving silences the voice of the enemy and amplifies the voice of God in your life.

The Bible says in Philippians 4:6, "Be anxious for nothing, but in everything by prayer and supplication, with thanksgiving, let your requests be made known to God." Thanksgiving is the weapon that defeats anxiety. When you thank God in the midst of your trials, you are declaring that He is bigger than your problems and faithful to bring you through.

Praise goes even further. While thanksgiving is about what God does, praise is about who God is. When you praise God for His character—His faithfulness, His power, His love, His wisdom—you align yourself with His nature, and His nature begins to manifest in your life.

The Covenant of Praise and Thanksgiving also releases supernatural joy. The Bible says the joy of the Lord is your strength. When you praise God, joy floods your soul, and that joy becomes the strength you need to overcome every obstacle.

Walking in this covenant requires intentionality. Make thanksgiving and praise a daily habit, not just something you do when things are going well. Thank God in advance for what He is about to do. Praise Him in the storm, knowing that He is working everything together for your good.

Today, enter His gates with thanksgiving and His courts with praise. As you worship, watch breakthrough manifest in every area of your life!

PROPHETIC DECLARATIONS

1. I declare that praise and thanksgiving are unlocking God's presence, power, and provision in my life right now!

2. I declare that as I enter His gates with thanksgiving and His courts with praise, I am positioning myself for supernatural breakthrough!

3. I declare that I am shifting my focus from my circumstances to God's goodness, and thanksgiving is silencing the voice of the enemy!

4. I declare that thanksgiving is defeating anxiety in my life, and I am declaring that God is bigger than my problems!

5. I declare that as I praise God for who He is, His nature is manifesting in my life—His faithfulness, power, love, and wisdom!

6. I declare that the joy of the Lord is my strength, and as I praise Him, supernatural joy is flooding my soul!
7. I declare that I am making thanksgiving and praise a daily habit, not just something I do when things are going well!
8. I declare that I am thanking God in advance for what He is about to do and praising Him in the storm!
9. I declare that worship is my weapon, thanksgiving is my shield, and praise is my pathway to victory!
10. I declare that the Covenant of Praise and Thanksgiving is activated over my life, and breakthrough is manifesting in every area right now in Jesus' name!

In Jesus' mighty name, AMEN!

16

COVENANT OF INCREASE

"I will multiply them, and they shall not diminish; I will also glorify them, and they shall not be small."

– Jeremiah 30:19 (NKJV) –

God's plan for you is not maintenance—it's multiplication. The Covenant of Increase declares that you are designed to grow, expand, and multiply in every area of your life. You will not diminish, decrease, or become insignificant. Instead, you will be glorified and magnified by the hand of God.

The prophet Jeremiah spoke these words to a nation that had been reduced, defeated, and exiled. But God promised that their season of decrease was ending and their season of increase was beginning. What was true for Israel is true for you—no matter what season of decrease you've experienced, God is about to multiply you.

The word "multiply" means to increase exponentially, not just incrementally. This is not about small, gradual growth. This is about supernatural acceleration where things that should take years happen in months, and opportunities that seemed impossible suddenly become available.

Notice the double promise: "They shall not diminish" and "they shall not be small." God is not only increasing you; He is also protecting you from decrease. The enemy may try to reduce your influence, shrink your resources, or limit your impact, but God's covenant guarantees that you will not be diminished. You are covered by divine protection that prevents loss and ensures increase.

This covenant applies to every area of your life. Your finances will increase. Your influence will expand. Your ministry will grow. Your family will be blessed. Your anointing will multiply. Your joy will abound. Your wisdom will deepen. There is no area of your life that God wants to remain stagnant.

The key to walking in the Covenant of Increase is expectation. You must see yourself increasing before you see it in the natural. Speak increase over your life. Pray for multiplication. Position yourself for growth. Sow seeds expecting a harvest. When you align your expectations with God's promises, increase becomes inevitable.

God also says, "I will glorify them, and they shall not be small." This means you will be honored, recognized, and celebrated. Your influence will expand beyond your local sphere. Your name will be known for good. Your impact will be significant. You are moving from obscurity to visibility, from insignificance to influence.

Today, declare that you are entering your season of increase. Decrease is over. Stagnation is broken. Multiplication is your portion. The Covenant of Increase is activated, and you are growing in every direction!

PROPHETIC DECLARATIONS

1. I declare that God's plan for me is multiplication, not maintenance—I am designed to grow, expand, and increase in every area!
2. I declare that I will not diminish, decrease, or become insignificant—I am being glorified and magnified by God's hand!
3. I declare that my season of decrease is over, and my season of supernatural increase has begun right now!
4. I declare that I am experiencing exponential multiplication—things that should take years are happening in months!

5. I declare that the enemy cannot reduce my influence, shrink my resources, or limit my impact—I am protected from decrease!

6. I declare that my finances are increasing, my influence is expanding, my ministry is growing, and my family is blessed!

7. I declare that I see myself increasing before I see it in the natural, and I align my expectations with God's promises!

8. I declare that I am sowing seeds expecting a harvest, positioning myself for growth, and speaking increase over my life!

9. I declare that I am moving from obscurity to visibility, from insignificance to influence—my impact will be significant!

10. I declare that the Covenant of Increase is activated over my life, and I am growing, multiplying, and expanding in every direction in Jesus' name!

In Jesus' mighty name, AMEN!

17

COVENANT OF FEASTS

And in this mountain the LORD of hosts will make for all people a feast of choice pieces, a feast of wines on the lees, of fat things full of marrow, of well-refined wines on the lees.

– Isaiah 25:6 (NKJV) –

God is not interested in giving you leftovers—He wants to give you the best! The Covenant of Feasts promises that God will prepare a table before you filled with choice pieces, the finest provisions, and the richest blessings. You are not destined for crumbs; you are invited to a feast!

The imagery in this verse is powerful. A feast represents abundance, celebration, joy, and satisfaction. It's not a quick snack or a simple meal—it's an extravagant banquet where nothing is lacking and everything is excellent. This is how God wants to bless you—not sparingly, but abundantly.

Notice the quality of what God provides: "choice pieces," "fat things full of marrow," and "well-refined wines." These represent the best of the best. God is not giving you second-rate blessings. He is giving you premium provisions, top-tier opportunities, and first-class favor. When God blesses you, He does it with excellence.

Many believers settle for less than God's best because they don't believe they deserve a feast. They've been conditioned to expect struggle, lack, and barely enough. But God wants to break that mentality and introduce you to His abundant table where there is always more than enough.

This covenant is for "all people"—meaning it's not exclusive to a select few. Every believer who comes to God's mountain can partake of His feast. You don't have to be perfect, wealthy, or influential to receive God's abundance. You just have to come to His table with faith and expectation.

The feast also represents spiritual nourishment. God wants to feed your soul with His presence, His Word, His joy, and His peace. When you feast on spiritual things, you are strengthened, satisfied, and empowered to walk in victory.

Walking in this covenant requires a shift in your mindset. Stop expecting barely enough and start expecting abundance. Stop settling for crumbs and start claiming your place at God's table. Stop living like a beggar and start living like a beloved child invited to the Father's banquet.

Today, God is preparing a feast for you. Come to His table with expectation. Receive His abundant blessings. Feast on His goodness. The Covenant of Feasts is yours, and you are moving from lack to abundance, from struggle to celebration!

PROPHETIC DECLARATIONS

1. I declare that God is preparing a feast for me filled with choice pieces, finest provisions, and richest blessings!
2. I declare that I am not destined for crumbs—I am invited to God's abundant banquet where nothing is lacking!
3. I declare that God is giving me premium provisions, top-tier opportunities, and first-class favor—the best of the best!
4. I declare that I am breaking the mentality of lack and stepping into God's abundant table where there is more than enough!

5. I declare that I don't have to be perfect to receive God's abundance—I come to His table with faith and expectation!

6. I declare that God is feeding my soul with His presence, His Word, His joy, and His peace, and I am spiritually satisfied!

7. I declare that I am shifting my mindset from barely enough to abundance, from crumbs to feasts, from begging to receiving!

8. I declare that I am not living like a beggar—I am living like a beloved child invited to the Father's extravagant banquet!

9. I declare that I am feasting on God's goodness, receiving His blessings with thanksgiving, and celebrating His abundance!

10. I declare that the Covenant of Feasts is activated over my life, and I am moving from lack to abundance, from struggle to celebration in Jesus' name!

In Jesus' mighty name, AMEN!

18

COVENANT OF JOY, LAUGHTER, AND ANSWERED PRAYERS

"Even them I will bring to My holy mountain, and make them joyful in My house of prayer. Their burnt offerings and their sacrifices will be accepted on My altar; for My house shall be called a house of prayer for all nations."

– Isaiah 56:7 (NKJV) –

God's house is not a place of sorrow and heaviness—it's a place of joy, laughter, and answered prayers! The Covenant of Joy, Laughter, and Answered Prayers declares that when you come into God's presence, you will experience supernatural joy and see your prayers answered.

The text says God will "make them joyful." This is not natural happiness that depends on circumstances; this is supernatural joy that God produces in your spirit. When you enter His house with expectation, God fills you with a joy that overcomes depression, defeats discouragement, and empowers you to face any challenge.

Notice that this joy is connected to prayer. God's house is called "a house of prayer," and in that house, prayers are answered. Your offerings and sacrifices are accepted, meaning God hears you and responds to you. When you pray, you are not talking to the ceiling—you are talking to a Father who listens and acts on your behalf.

The Covenant of Joy, Laughter, and Answered Prayers also includes restoration of laughter. Job 8:21 says, "He will yet fill your mouth with laughter, and your lips with rejoicing." If the enemy has stolen your laughter through trials, losses, or disappointments, God is restoring it right now. You will laugh again. You will celebrate again. You will rejoice again.

Laughter is a weapon against the enemy. Psalm 2:4 says, "He who sits in the heavens shall laugh; the Lord shall hold them in derision." When you laugh in faith, you are declaring that God is bigger than your problems and that victory is already yours. Laughter releases stress, heals your body, and lifts your spirit.

Answered prayer is also part of this covenant. God is not deaf to your cries. He hears every prayer you've prayed, and He is working behind the scenes to bring them to pass. Some answers will come quickly; others will take time. But rest assured, no prayer offered in faith goes unanswered.

Today, enter God's house with expectation. Bring your burdens to Him in prayer, and receive His joy in exchange. Allow laughter to fill your mouth and rejoicing to fill your heart. Your prayers are being answered, and joy is your portion!

PROPHETIC DECLARATIONS

1. I declare that God's house is a place of joy, laughter, and answered prayers, and I am experiencing all three right now!
2. I declare that God is making me joyful—supernatural joy is overcoming depression, defeating discouragement, and empowering me!
3. I declare that my prayers are being heard and answered because God's house is a house of prayer for all nations!
4. I declare that my offerings and sacrifices are accepted, and God is responding to my prayers on my behalf!
5. I declare that laughter is being restored to my life—I will laugh again, celebrate again, and rejoice again!

6. I declare that laughter is my weapon against the enemy, and I am laughing in faith knowing that victory is already mine!

7. I declare that laughter is releasing stress from my body, healing my emotions, and lifting my spirit in Jesus' name!

8. I declare that no prayer I've offered in faith goes unanswered—God is working behind the scenes to bring them to pass!

9. I declare that I am entering God's house with expectation, bringing my burdens in prayer, and receiving His joy in exchange!

10. I declare that the Covenant of Joy, Laughter, and Answered Prayers is activated over my life, and breakthrough is manifesting now!

In Jesus' mighty name, AMEN!

19

COVENANT OF THE LORD'S MOUNTAIN

Now it shall come to pass in the latter days that the mountain of the LORD's house shall be established on the top of the mountains, and shall be exalted above the hills; and all nations shall flow to it. Many people shall come and say, "Come, and let us go up to the mountain of the LORD, to the house of the God of Jacob; He will teach us His ways, and we shall walk in His paths." For out of Zion shall go forth the law, and the word of the LORD from Jerusalem.

– Isaiah 2:2-3 (NKJV) –

The Covenant of the Lord's Mountain is a promise of elevation, influence, and divine instruction. God is establishing His house—His presence and His people—on the top of the mountains, meaning you will be positioned above every obstacle, every challenge, and every opposition.

Mountains in Scripture represent kingdoms, governments, and spheres of influence. When God says His mountain will be established "on the top of the mountains," He is declaring that His kingdom will have supremacy over every other kingdom. As a believer, you are part of God's kingdom, and that means you are positioned for influence and authority.

The phrase "exalted above the hills" means you will not be hidden or overlooked. You will be visible, recognized, and sought after. The text says "all nations shall flow to it," meaning people will come to you for wisdom, guidance, and blessing. You are being positioned as a source of light in a dark world.

Notice what draws people to the mountain: "He will teach us His ways, and we shall walk in His paths." God is making you a teacher, a guide, a mentor, and an example. Your life will demonstrate God's wisdom, and people will want what you have. Your testimony will attract others to the Lord.

This covenant also includes divine instruction. God says, "Out of Zion shall go forth the law, and the word of the LORD." You are not left to figure out life on your own. God is giving you clear direction, divine wisdom, and supernatural insight for every decision you face. His Word will guide your steps and His Spirit will lead you into all truth.

Walking in this covenant requires humility and faithfulness. God elevates those who remain humble before Him and faithful in small things. As you serve God faithfully where you are, He will elevate you to where He wants you to be.

Today, declare that you are being positioned on the top of the mountains. You are being exalted above the hills. Your influence is expanding, and nations are flowing to you for wisdom and blessing. The Covenant of the Lord's Mountain is yours!

PROPHETIC DECLARATIONS

1. I declare that I am being positioned on the top of the mountains—above every obstacle, challenge, and opposition!
2. I declare that God's kingdom has supremacy over every other kingdom, and I walk in authority and influence as part of His kingdom!
3. I declare that I am being exalted above the hills—I am visible, recognized, and sought after for wisdom and blessing!
4. I declare that people are flowing to me for guidance, and my life is demonstrating God's wisdom to a dark world!

5. I declare that I am a teacher, guide, mentor, and example, and my testimony is attracting others to the Lord!

6. I declare that God is giving me clear direction, divine wisdom, and supernatural insight for every decision I face!

7. I declare that God's Word is guiding my steps, and His Spirit is leading me into all truth!

8. I declare that I remain humble before God and faithful in small things, and He is elevating me to new levels of influence!

9. I declare that my sphere of influence is expanding, and I am positioned as a source of light and hope!

10. I declare that the Covenant of the Lord's Mountain is activated over my life, and I am walking in divine elevation and authority in Jesus' name!

In Jesus' mighty name, AMEN!

20

COVENANT OF MASSIVE HARVEST

Then I raised my eyes and looked, and behold, a man with a measuring line in his hand. So I said, "Where are you going?" And he said to me, "To measure Jerusalem, to see what is its width and what is its length."

– Zechariah 2:1-2 (NKJV) –

God is measuring the increase that is coming to your life. The Covenant of Massive Harvest declares that God is preparing space for the abundance He is about to release. Your capacity is being expanded, your borders are being enlarged, and your harvest is about to exceed your expectations.

In this vision, the angel is measuring Jerusalem to determine its dimensions. But why measure? Because God was about to expand the city beyond its current capacity.

New people were coming, new blessings were arriving, and new opportunities were opening. The measuring represented preparation for massive increase.

God is doing the same thing in your life. He is measuring the space you currently occupy—spiritually, financially, relationally, and professionally—and He is preparing to expand it. What you have now is too small for what God is about to do. Your current capacity cannot contain the harvest that is coming.

The Covenant of Massive Harvest means you will reap more than you sowed. You will receive more than you expected. You will experience increase that seems disproportionate to your efforts. This is because God is adding His supernatural blessing to your natural labor, and the result is exponential multiplication.

This harvest includes every area of your life. Financially, you will see income increase from multiple sources. Relationally, you will experience deeper connections and meaningful relationships. Spiritually, you will encounter God at new levels of intimacy and power. Professionally, you will advance beyond your current position into greater influence and authority.

But harvest requires preparation. You must prepare your heart to receive, prepare your hands to work, and prepare your mind to manage increase. Expanding capacity means expanding your faith, your vision, and your stewardship. As you prepare, God will pour out blessings you don't have room enough to contain.

The Bible says in Malachi 3:10, "Bring all the tithes into the storehouse...and try Me now in this...if I will not open for you the windows of heaven and pour out for you such blessing that there will not be room enough to receive it." This is the Covenant of Massive Harvest—overflow, abundance, and more than enough.

Today, declare that your harvest is coming. Your capacity is expanding. Your borders are being enlarged. Get ready to receive the massive harvest God has prepared for you!

PROPHETIC DECLARATIONS

1. I declare that God is measuring the increase that is coming to my life, and my capacity is being expanded for massive harvest!

2. I declare that my borders are being enlarged, and what I have now is too small for what God is about to do!

3. I declare that I will reap more than I sowed, receive more than I expected, and experience increase beyond my efforts!

4. I declare that God's supernatural blessing is multiplying my natural labor, and the result is exponential increase!

5. I declare that my harvest includes every area—finances, relationships, spiritual growth, and professional advancement!

6. I declare that income is increasing from multiple sources, and I am experiencing financial breakthrough right now!

7. I declare that I am preparing my heart to receive, my hands to work, and my mind to manage the increase God is sending!

8. I declare that I am expanding my faith, my vision, and my stewardship to handle the massive harvest coming my way!

9. I declare that the windows of heaven are opening over my life, and blessings are pouring out that I don't have room to contain!

10. I declare that the Covenant of Massive Harvest is activated over my life—overflow, abundance, and more than enough in Jesus' name!

In Jesus' mighty name, AMEN!

21

COVENANT OF HOLINESS AND RIGHTEOUSNESS UNTO THE LORD

"And you shall be to Me a kingdom of priests and a holy nation." These are the words which you shall speak to the children of Israel.

– Exodus 19:6 (NKJV) –

God has called you to be set apart for His purposes. The Covenant of Holiness and Righteousness unto the Lord declares that you are not ordinary—you are a kingdom of priests and a holy nation. You belong to God, and you represent Him on the earth.

Holiness means being set apart for God's exclusive use. It's not about perfectionism or legalism; it's about consecration and dedication. When you walk in holiness, you are saying, "God, my life is Yours. My body is Your temple. My time is Your investment. My resources are Your tools. I am set apart for Your glory."

Notice that God calls you "a kingdom of priests." In the Old Testament, only certain people could serve as priests and enter God's presence. But under the New Covenant, every believer is a priest with direct access to God. You don't need a mediator to approach God. You can come boldly to His throne and minister to Him in worship, prayer, and service.

Being "a holy nation" means you are part of a unique people who live by God's standards, not the world's standards. The world promotes compromise, but you promote righteousness. The world pursues pleasure, but you pursue purity. The world seeks approval, but you seek God's acceptance.

Righteousness is not about your own efforts to be good; it's about receiving Christ's righteousness by faith. When you accepted Jesus, His righteousness was credited to your account. Now you are the righteousness of God in Christ. You don't strive to become righteous—you walk in the righteousness you already possess.

Walking in holiness and righteousness doesn't make you boring or irrelevant. It makes you powerful and influential. When you live a consecrated life, God's presence rests on you, His favor surrounds you, and His power flows through you. People will be drawn to the light in you because they see something different, something authentic, something supernatural.

This covenant also includes protection. Holiness is a hedge of protection around your life. When you live set apart for God, the enemy has limited access to you. Sin opens doors to the enemy, but holiness closes those doors and keeps you safe in God's will.

Today, consecrate yourself afresh to the Lord. Declare that you are a kingdom of priests and a holy nation. Choose holiness over compromise, righteousness over sin, and God's approval over the world's acceptance. The Covenant of Holiness and Righteousness is yours!

PROPHETIC DECLARATIONS

1. I declare that I am set apart for God's purposes—I am a kingdom of priests and a holy nation unto the Lord!
2. I declare that my life belongs to God, and I am consecrated and dedicated for His exclusive use and glory!
3. I declare that I have direct access to God as a priest under the New Covenant, and I come boldly to His throne!

4. I declare that I am part of a unique people who live by God's standards, not the world's standards!

5. I declare that I am the righteousness of God in Christ, and I walk in the righteousness I already possess by faith!

6. I declare that walking in holiness makes me powerful and influential—God's presence rests on me and His favor surrounds me!

7. I declare that people are drawn to the light in me because they see something different, authentic, and supernatural!

8. I declare that holiness is a hedge of protection around my life, and the enemy has limited access to me!

9. I declare that I choose holiness over compromise, righteousness over sin, and God's approval over the world's acceptance!

10. I declare that the Covenant of Holiness and Righteousness unto the Lord is activated over my life, and I am walking in consecration and power in Jesus' name!

In Jesus' mighty name, AMEN!

22

COVENANT OF GOD'S SPIRIT AND HIS COVENANT WORD IN US

"As for Me," says the LORD, "this is My covenant with them: My Spirit who is upon you, and My words which I have put in your mouth, shall not depart from your mouth, nor from the mouth of your descendants, nor from the mouth of your descendants' descendants," says the LORD, "from this time and forevermore."

– Isaiah 59:21 (NKJV) –

The greatest treasure you possess is not in your bank account—it's God's Spirit upon you and God's Word in you. The Covenant of God's Spirit and His Covenant Word in Us guarantees that the Holy Spirit will never leave you and God's Word will never depart from your mouth.

This is a generational covenant. God is not just making a promise to you; He is making a promise to your children and your children's children. The Spirit and the Word will remain in your family line from this time and forevermore. What a powerful legacy to leave!

God's Spirit upon you means you have divine power, divine guidance, divine comfort, and divine transformation available to you every moment of every day. The Holy Spirit is your helper, your teacher, your advocate, and your friend. He is with you in every situation, empowering you to live victoriously.

God's Word in your mouth means you carry divine authority. The Bible says in Proverbs 18:21, "Death and life are in the power of the tongue." When you speak God's Word, you are releasing creative power that changes circumstances, heals bodies, opens doors, and defeats enemies. Your words have weight when they align with God's Word.

Many believers underestimate the power of speaking God's Word. They speak their problems more than they speak God's promises. They declare their fears more than they declare their faith. But this covenant calls you to fill your mouth with God's Word so that every word you speak carries divine authority.

The phrase "shall not depart" means the Spirit and the Word will be constant companions in your life. You won't have seasons where the Spirit leaves or the Word becomes irrelevant. They will remain with you through every trial, every transition, and every triumph.

Walking in this covenant requires intentionality. You must spend time in God's Word daily, allowing it to saturate your mind and heart. You must yield to the Holy Spirit's promptings, following His guidance and obeying His voice. As you do, the Spirit and the Word will transform you into the image of Christ.

Today, declare that God's Spirit is upon you and God's Word is in your mouth. You carry divine power and divine authority. You are speaking life, declaring breakthrough, and releasing God's will on earth!

PROPHETIC DECLARATIONS

1. I declare that God's Spirit is upon me and God's Word is in my mouth—this covenant will never depart from me!
2. I declare that this is a generational covenant—God's Spirit and Word will remain in my family line forevermore!
3. I declare that the Holy Spirit is my helper, teacher, advocate, and friend, empowering me to live victoriously every day!

4. I declare that I carry divine authority because God's Word is in my mouth, and my words have creative power!

5. I declare that I am speaking God's promises more than my problems and declaring my faith more than my fears!

6. I declare that the Spirit and the Word are constant companions in my life, remaining with me through every season!

7. I declare that I am spending time in God's Word daily, allowing it to saturate my mind and transform my heart!

8. I declare that I am yielding to the Holy Spirit's promptings, following His guidance, and obeying His voice!

9. I declare that I am speaking life, declaring breakthrough, and releasing God's will on earth through the power of my words!

10. I declare that the Covenant of God's Spirit and His Covenant Word in Us is activated over my life and my family, and we are walking in divine power and authority in Jesus' name!

In Jesus' mighty name, AMEN!

23

COVENANT OF DIVINE REMEMBRANCE

Then those who feared the LORD spoke to one another, and the LORD listened and heard them; so a book of remembrance was written before Him for those who fear the LORD and who meditate on His name.

– Malachi 3:16 (NKJV) –

God keeps records of your faithfulness. The Covenant of Divine Remembrance assures you that every act of obedience, every prayer you've prayed, every seed you've sown, and every sacrifice you've made is recorded in heaven. Nothing you do for God goes unnoticed or unrewarded.

The phrase "a book of remembrance was written before Him" is powerful. God has a book with your name in it, and in that book, He records everything you do in faith.

Every time you worship when you don't feel like it, every time you give when it's difficult, every time you serve when you're tired—God writes it down.

This covenant is specifically for "those who fear the LORD and who meditate on His name." Fearing the Lord means reverencing Him, honoring Him, and making Him the priority of your life. Meditating on His name means thinking about His character, declaring His attributes, and focusing on who He is. When you do these things, you activate divine remembrance.

Many believers feel forgotten. They've served faithfully for years, given sacrificially, and prayed consistently, yet they see no visible results. But God wants you to know that He sees everything, He remembers everything, and He will reward everything. Your labor is not in vain in the Lord.

The Bible says in Hebrews 6:10, "For God is not unjust to forget your work and labor of love which you have shown toward His name." God doesn't forget. He doesn't overlook. He doesn't ignore. He remembers, and at the appointed time, He rewards.

This covenant also means that your legacy is secure. Even after you're gone, God remembers what you did for His kingdom. Your faithfulness impacts generations, and your obedience creates pathways for your descendants. The book of remembrance ensures that your life counts for eternity.

Walking in this covenant requires consistency. Don't grow weary in doing good. Don't give up when results seem delayed. Don't stop serving when recognition doesn't come. Keep fearing the Lord, keep meditating on His name, and keep trusting that God is recording everything in His book.

Today, be encouraged! God has not forgotten you. Your faithfulness is recorded in heaven. Your rewards are coming. The Covenant of Divine Remembrance is working on your behalf right now!

PROPHETIC DECLARATIONS

1. I declare that God keeps records of my faithfulness, and every act of obedience is recorded in heaven!
2. I declare that nothing I do for God goes unnoticed or unrewarded—He sees everything and remembers everything!
3. I declare that God has a book of remembrance with my name in it, and He is recording every act of worship, giving, and service!

4. I declare that I fear the LORD and meditate on His name, and I am activating divine remembrance over my life!

5. I declare that I am not forgotten—God sees my faithfulness, remembers my sacrifices, and will reward my labor of love!

6. I declare that God is not unjust to forget my work and labor of love toward His name—my rewards are coming!

7. I declare that my legacy is secure because God remembers what I do for His kingdom, impacting future generations!

8. I declare that I will not grow weary in doing good—I will keep fearing the Lord and trusting His perfect timing!

9. I declare that I am consistent in my faithfulness, and God is working on my behalf even when I don't see results!

10. I declare that the Covenant of Divine Remembrance is activated over my life, and my rewards are being released from heaven now in Jesus' name!

In Jesus' mighty name, AMEN!

24

COVENANT OF DIVINE VENGEANCE

Beloved, do not avenge yourselves, but rather give place to wrath; for it is written, "Vengeance is Mine, I will repay," says the Lord.

– Romans 12:19 (NKJV) –

You don't have to fight your own battles. The Covenant of Divine Vengeance declares that God will fight for you, vindicate you, and repay everyone who has wronged you. Your responsibility is to forgive, and God's responsibility is to bring justice.

This covenant is a relief for those who have been hurt, betrayed, or mistreated. The natural response to injustice is revenge—we want to hurt those who hurt us. But God says, "Don't avenge yourselves. Give place to My wrath. I will handle it." When you release your offenders to God, you position yourself to receive His divine justice.

Notice the phrase "give place to wrath." This means you step back and let God step in. You stop plotting revenge and start trusting God's timing. You stop seeking retaliation and start seeking God's will. When you give place to God's wrath, you are acknowledging that He is a better judge than you and a more effective avenger.

The promise "I will repay" is God's guarantee that He will settle the score. You don't have to worry about whether justice will be served. God sees everything that was done to you, and He will make it right. His repayment may not look like what you expect, but it will be perfect, complete, and satisfying.

This covenant also protects you from the sin of bitterness and unforgiveness. When you hold onto offense, you poison your own soul. But when you release your offenders to God, you free yourself from the burden of anger, resentment, and revenge. Forgiveness is not excusing what they did; it's trusting God to handle it.

The Bible says in Deuteronomy 32:35, "Vengeance is Mine, and recompense; their foot shall slip in due time." God's timing is perfect. He will deal with your enemies at the right time, in the right way, for the right reasons. You don't have to rush the process or force the outcome. Trust God's timing and rest in His justice.

Walking in this covenant requires humility and faith. You must humble yourself under God's mighty hand and trust that He will exalt you in due time. You must have faith that God's justice is better than your revenge. As you walk this way, you experience peace, freedom, and supernatural vindication.

Today, release every offense to God. Let go of the need for revenge. Trust that God will repay. The Covenant of Divine Vengeance is working on your behalf, and God is fighting your battles!

PROPHETIC DECLARATIONS

1. I declare that I don't have to fight my own battles—God is fighting for me, vindicating me, and repaying everyone who wronged me!
2. I declare that I am releasing my offenders to God, and I am positioning myself to receive His divine justice!
3. I declare that I am giving place to God's wrath—I step back so God can step in and settle every score!
4. I declare that God sees everything that was done to me, and He will make it right in His perfect timing!
5. I declare that I am free from bitterness and unforgiveness—I forgive those who hurt me and trust God to handle it!

6. I declare that God's repayment is perfect, complete, and satisfying, and I am trusting His justice over my revenge!
7. I declare that God's timing is perfect, and He will deal with my enemies at the right time, in the right way!
8. I declare that I am walking in humility and faith, trusting that God will exalt me in due time!
9. I declare that I am experiencing peace, freedom, and supernatural vindication as I release every offense to God!
10. I declare that the Covenant of Divine Vengeance is activated over my life, and God is fighting my battles right now in Jesus' mighty name!

In Jesus' mighty name, AMEN!

25

COVENANT OF FRUITFULNESS

Then God blessed them, and God said to them, "Be fruitful and multiply; fill the earth and subdue it; have dominion over the fish of the sea, over the birds of the air, and over every living thing that moves on the earth."

– Genesis 1:28 (NKJV) –

The first command God gave to humanity was not "be holy" or "worship Me"—it was "be fruitful." The Covenant of Fruitfulness declares that you were created to produce, multiply, and exercise dominion. Barrenness, stagnation, and unproductivity are not God's will for your life.

To be fruitful means to produce results in every area of your life. Spiritual fruitfulness means growing in the fruit of the Spirit—love, joy, peace, patience, kindness, goodness, faithfulness, gentleness, and self-control. Relational fruitfulness means building healthy, life-giving connections. Financial fruitfulness means increasing your resources and stewarding them wisely. Ministry fruitfulness means impacting lives for the kingdom of God.

The command to "multiply" means you won't stay where you are. What you have now will increase. What you do now will expand. What you see now will multiply. This is God's original design for your life—constant growth, continual increase, and consistent multiplication.

God also commanded humanity to "fill the earth and subdue it." This means you are called to take territory, not retreat from it. You are called to advance, not hide. You are called to influence, not be influenced. The enemy wants to limit your impact, but God wants you to fill the earth with His glory through your life.

The phrase "have dominion" means you were created to rule, not be ruled. You have authority over circumstances, authority over the enemy, and authority to create change. Don't live as a victim of your environment—live as a victor who exercises dominion over it.

Fruitfulness is not automatic. Jesus said in John 15:5, "I am the vine, you are the branches. He who abides in Me, and I in him, bears much fruit; for without Me you can do nothing." The key to fruitfulness is abiding in Christ. When you stay connected to Him through prayer, worship, and obedience, fruitfulness flows naturally.

This covenant also breaks every curse of barrenness. If you've been struggling with unproductivity in any area—relationships, finances, ministry, career—God is breaking that curse right now. You are entering your season of fruitfulness, and you will produce, multiply, and have dominion!

Today, declare that barrenness is over. Stagnation is broken. Fruitfulness is your portion. You are producing in every area, multiplying in every direction, and exercising dominion over every challenge!

PROPHETIC DECLARATIONS

1. I declare that I was created to be fruitful, and barrenness, stagnation, and unproductivity are not God's will for me!

2. I declare that I am producing results in every area—spiritual growth, healthy relationships, financial increase, and kingdom impact!

3. I declare that I am multiplying—what I have now will increase, what I do now will expand, and what I see now will multiply!

4. I declare that I am taking territory, advancing forward, and filling the earth with God's glory through my life!

5. I declare that I have dominion over circumstances, authority over the enemy, and power to create change in Jesus' name!
6. I declare that I am not a victim of my environment—I am a victor who exercises dominion over every challenge!
7. I declare that I am abiding in Christ, staying connected through prayer, worship, and obedience, and fruitfulness flows naturally!
8. I declare that every curse of barrenness is broken off my life—I am entering my season of supernatural fruitfulness!
9. I declare that I am producing, multiplying, and having dominion in my relationships, finances, ministry, and career!
10. I declare that the Covenant of Fruitfulness is activated over my life, and I am bearing much fruit in every area right now in Jesus' name!

In Jesus' mighty name, AMEN!

26

COVENANT OF PRAISE ON THE EARTH

"At that time I will bring you back, even at the time I gather you; for I will give you fame and praise among all the peoples of the earth, when I return your captives before your eyes," says the LORD.

– Zephaniah 3:20 (NKJV) –

God is about to turn your story around and give you fame and praise among all peoples. The Covenant of Praise on the Earth declares that what the enemy stole from you will be returned, and when it is, everyone will see God's faithfulness in your life. Your testimony will become your platform for praise.

This verse is God's promise to restore what was lost. The phrase "I will return your captives before your eyes" means you will personally witness your breakthrough. You won't just hear about it; you will see it with your own eyes. Everything the enemy took—your peace, your joy, your health, your finances, your relationships—God is bringing back.

But restoration is not the end of the story. God says, "I will give you fame and praise among all the peoples of the earth." This means your restoration will be so remarkable that people will talk about it. Your comeback will be so powerful that it will bring glory to God. Your testimony will be so compelling that it will inspire faith in others.

This is not about seeking recognition for yourself; it's about God receiving praise through your life. When people see what God has done for you, they will praise Him. When they hear your testimony, they will glorify Him. Your life becomes a display of God's power, faithfulness, and goodness.

The Covenant of Praise on the Earth also means your influence will expand beyond your local sphere. God will use your story to impact cities, nations, and even the world. What you've been through was not just for you—it was preparing you to be a voice of hope for others.

Walking in this covenant requires boldness to share your testimony. Don't hide what God has done. Don't minimize your breakthrough. Don't be ashamed of your past. Share your story with confidence, knowing that God is using it to set others free and bring praise to His name.

Today is the final day of this devotional journey, but it's the beginning of your breakthrough season. You've read 26 covenant promises, and now it's time to walk in them. Declare every promise over your life, believe God for the impossible, and watch Him turn your captivity into praise.

The Lord is bringing you back, gathering you in, and giving you fame and praise. Your season of mourning is over. Your season of restoration has come. Your testimony will bring glory to God and hope to the world. The Covenant of Praise on the Earth is yours—receive it now in Jesus' name!

PROPHETIC DECLARATIONS

1. I declare that God is turning my story around and giving me fame and praise among all peoples of the earth!
2. I declare that everything the enemy stole from me is being returned, and I will witness my breakthrough with my own eyes!
3. I declare that my restoration is so remarkable that people will talk about it and give glory to God!
4. I declare that my comeback is so powerful that it will inspire faith in others and bring praise to God's name!

5. I declare that my life is a display of God's power, faithfulness, and goodness, and people are seeing His glory in me!

6. I declare that my influence is expanding beyond my local sphere, impacting cities, nations, and the world!

7. I declare that I am boldly sharing my testimony, and God is using my story to set others free!

8. I declare that I am not ashamed of my past—I am confident in God's restoration and the praise it brings to His name!

9. I declare that this is my breakthrough season—I am walking in all 26 covenant promises and believing God for the impossible!

10. I declare that the Covenant of Praise on the Earth is activated over my life—my season of mourning is over, my restoration has come, and my testimony will bring glory to God and hope to the world in Jesus' mighty name!

In Jesus' mighty name, AMEN!

CONCLUSION

You have journeyed through 26 Covenant Promises for Open Heaven. Each promise is not just a nice thought—it is a divine guarantee backed by the faithfulness of God. As you go forward, remember that these covenants are not dependent on your perfection but on God's unchanging nature.

Make these declarations daily. Meditate on these scriptures regularly. Walk in faith constantly. Your breakthrough is not a matter of "if" but "when," and that "when" is now. God is too faithful to fail, and His covenant promises will manifest in your life.

May the God of all grace, who has called you to His eternal glory in Christ, establish, strengthen, settle, and perfect you. May you walk in open heavens, supernatural supply, divine protection, and every covenant blessing that belongs to you. May your latter glory be greater than your former, and may your life bring praise to God on the earth.

In Jesus' mighty name, AMEN!

www.ingramcontent.com/pod-product-compliance
Lightning Source LLC
LaVergne TN
LVHW010935110826
845149LV00013B/2606

* 9 7 8 1 9 6 5 5 9 3 7 8 3 *